The Sinfulness of Sin

Surrender Ministries

© Matthew Munro and Blake Wiley 2014

ESV Copyright and Permissions Information

The Holy Bible, English Standard Version® (ESV®)

Copyright © 2001 by Crossway,

A publishing ministry of Good News Publishers.

All rights reserved.

ESV Text Edition: 2011

Table of Contents

Introduction 3

The Necessity of Damnation 5

The Curse of Damnation 8

The Grounds of Damnation 12

The Universality of Damnation 18

The End of Damnation 25

The Salvation From Damnation 28

Bibliography 30

Introduction

"Preach the word...for the time is coming when people will not endure sound teaching, but having itching ears they will accumulate for themselves teachers to suit their own passions."

- 2 Timothy 4:2, 3

We live in a world that is growing increasingly dark. Eastern religions are becoming increasingly popular in Western secular societies that all too easily embrace philosophies that remove all personal responsibilities. Humanistic beliefs about evolution abound, as do false forms of Christianity. The Gospel preached in a large number of churches is a watered down message of prosperous, easy life in this world with little word of the next. While the pastoral letters focused on preaching solid doctrine and truth, it seems most modern preachers are more concerned with crowds.

In keeping with this atmosphere of doctrinal ignorance, a popular preacher once told his congregation that Hell is not a literal place of torment, but rather an eternal state where one must live with their sins as they gradually grow worse. Such lunacy is blatantly unbiblical, yet was readily accepted. Added with the concept of "Your Best

Life Now", one must wonder where the confronting "offense of the cross" (Galatians 5:11) has disappeared to.

The book you are holding is a protest. Leonard Ravenhill once said, "we're more afraid of holiness than we are of sinfulness" (A Burning Heart), and that begins with a lack of solid understanding of the natural state of human beings. This book is not an extensive study of the doctrine of man, but it aims to provide a basic overview of man's creation, fall, and salvation.

The subject of this work is sin: its origin, its effect, its consequences, its defeat. In a series of studies into the biblical texts, the reader will see the horror of sin, and be able to contrast it with the beauty of God's mercy. It is the prayer of the authors that Christians will be strengthened in their walk with God as they come to a deeper appreciation for the Cross, and that sinners would receive salvation.

To God alone be the glory.

The Necessity of Damnation

"In the beginning, God created the heavens and the earth" (Genesis 1:1). Our God doesn't do things just for the sake of it. He had a purpose, a reason for what He did. Seven times in Genesis 1, God looked upon His creation and declared that it was 'good' – indeed, in verse 31, He saw it as 'very good'. The original Hebrew for this word 'good' indicates that it was not only good, but that it brought joy to God to look upon it. The stars and heavenly bodies separated day from night and marked the seasons (verse 14-19), the creatures and vegetation brought glory to God's power, and all was beautiful.

However, there was something missing in all this. While God's glory and ingenuity was beautifully reflected in creation, there was one more thing to be added, and so God created man in His own image (Genesis 1:26). That image indicates our eternal life, our intellect, will, emotions, free agency, and sense of morality. These things separate us from the rest of creation and show us to be the image of God. The natural result of this was that mankind was given dominion over creation (Genesis 1:29-30). We were granted authority over all nature on this earth, a sentiment that is echoed throughout the Bible, not just these opening verses.

At this point in history, everything was perfect, ideal, just what God had intended. There was no sin, no death, no decay, nothing to stain the perfection of God's hand.

That beautiful dominion, however, is what we corrupted when mankind fell. In Genesis 3, Satan entered into the serpent and used it to tempt Eve to break God's one commandment: "but of the tree of the knowledge of good and evil you shall not eat, for in the day that you eat of it you shall surely die." (Genesis 2:17). Genesis 3:6 tells us that Adam was standing beside Eve at this point. Right here, at the first temptation recorded in Scripture, the man had the opportunity to step in and say, "No. God made His commandment clear, and we will hold to that out of obedience to our Creator". Right here, Adam, in all his perfection, could have taken a stand and cast the devil out of this world.

Right here, Adam stayed silent. Eve ate the fruit, giving into temptation, then went to hand it to Adam. Once again, Adam could have stood for God and stayed pure. Once again, Adam stayed silent and just took a bite. They had everything they could have ever wanted – and everything we ourselves still want – and yet they fell to the temptation to do the one thing they were commanded not to. In that single, horrific moment, they revealed that, even in the midst of perfection, mankind is liable to destroy everything they were entrusted with.

As a result of this rebellion, the serpent was cursed, Adam and Eve were cursed, and mankind was banished from the Garden of Eden. It is generally believed that the Garden was destroyed in the global flood of Genesis 7. This is where sin, death, and decay entered the world. Because Adam and Eve, the authorities of Creation, fell, so too did what they were granted dominion over. Creation is now stuck in the bondage of decay, eagerly awaiting the final redemption (Romans 8:19-21).

Once that initial sin was committed, humanity allowed murder, infidelity, pride, and all kinds of sin into the world. The door was opened, and the devil took full advantage in order to corrupt the image of God within us, thus making us sons of darkness rather than children of God. Creation fell, and the necessity of damnation became clear.

The Curse of Damnation

Genesis 3:14-19

*The L*ORD *God said to the serpent,*

"Because you have done this,

cursed are you above all livestock

and above all beasts of the field;

on your belly you shall go,

and dust you shall eat

all the days of your life.

I will put enmity between you and the woman,

and between your offspring and her offspring;

he shall bruise your head,

and you shall bruise his heel."

To the woman he said,

"I will surely multiply your pain in childbearing;

in pain you shall bring forth children.

Your desire shall be for your husband,

and he shall rule over you."

And to Adam he said,

"Because you have listened to the voice of your wife

and have eaten of the tree

of which I commanded you,

'You shall not eat of it,'

cursed is the ground because of you;

in pain you shall eat of it all the days of your life;

thorns and thistles it shall bring forth for you;

and you shall eat the plants of the field.

By the sweat of your face

you shall eat bread,

till you return to the ground,

for out of it you were taken;

for you are dust,

and to dust you shall return."

In verse 14, God pronounces a curse on the physical serpent, condemning it to a life on its stomach in the dirt to represent the lowliness and filth that is brought about by the Fall. Take note that people also avoid snakes out of fear, as we should avoid sin out of fear.

In verse 15, God turns to the Devil. His curse is clear. Satan and his offspring – fallen, sinful humanity – will live in conflict with Godly men and women. They always have been, and always will be, in direct opposition to the purposes of God. Sinful humanity will always be opposed to the glory, praise, and honour of God. John MacArthur put it best: "mankind is hellbent on rebellion" (2011).

But there is hope here: the first Gospel account is in these verses: "he shall bruise your head, and you shall bruise his heel." These words appear to be referring to a specific conflict between the serpent and one particular human being. A few thousand years later, we understand that to be Jesus Christ. Satan bruised His heel at the Cross, when Christ was crucified for our salvation, but at the same moment, Christ bruised Satan's head and inflicted a fatal wound when He used such a death to conquer sin's dominion over humanity.

Woman is cursed to have pain in childbirth. She will now give birth to sinners, rebels, and have to watch as they fight against God. Man must now toil, labour, agonise, to have food to eat. Everything he obtains is obtained through blood, sweat, and tears. While man was always designed for work (see the commission in Genesis 2:15), it was originally a joy and pleasure. Only now that we live in rebellion to God's purposes does fulfilling them become a burden. It is still our obligation to work, by God's command, but we have, through our rebellion, lost our joy in doing so.

This is the curse that God placed on the Devil, and humanity. The out-workings are revealed throughout the Old Testament, and summarised in the New Testament.

The Grounds for Damnation

Romans 1:28-31

And since they did not see fit to acknowledge God, God gave them up to a debased mind to do what ought not to be done. They were filled with all manner of unrighteousness, evil, covetousness, malice. They are full of envy, murder, strife, deceit, maliciousness. They are gossips, slanderers, haters of God, insolent, haughty, boastful, inventors of evil, disobedient to parents, foolish, faithless, heartless, ruthless. Though they know God's righteous decree that those who practice such things deserve to die, they not only do them but give approval to those who practice them.

By this point mankind has rejected God's revelation, God's truth, and God's morality. Yet still even this decay has not satisfied our race's depravity. Here the most shocking foundation of humanity's rebellion is made clear: they did not think it worthwhile to retain the knowledge of God. Mankind has spat in God's face, entirely rejected Him, and decided that He is not worth remembering. Like the idols of Egypt, Greece, and Babylon, God is increasingly looked upon as an old concept not worth remembering. Those who live truly devoted to God are not praised and respected, but rather looked upon as utter fools. There is no love for God, and men are praised for how anti-Christ they are.

How different is the thought of the man of God! Let us never forget God's beautiful words through the prophet Jeremiah: "Let him who boasts boast about this: that he understands and knows me" (9:24). If humanity was created to know God, then surely our highest pursuit is to know God!

Yet there is a consequence to this treason. Those who are guilty will be given over to a depraved mind, to do what God forbids, what the Bible condemns. Those who go down that road of rejection can never turn back without a glorious work of the Holy Spirit. They will be trapped by the chains of their sins, and there will be no hope for them.

Note the procession of the crimes of wicked, depraved men. The first few attributes – wickedness, evil, greed and depravity – are against God Himself. They are wicked, in contradiction to God's demand for holiness. They are evil, in contradiction to God's goodness. They are full of greed, in contradiction to God's generosity. And they are full of depravity, as opposed to holiness. The sinner is first acting against God Himself, and then this spreads into sin against his neighbour. Envy of what others have, murder to receive it, strife instead of reconciliation, deceit for personal gain, malice in place of love, gossips instead of constructive, faithful friends.

Once a man despises God, he despises what God is, and what God has created. Rather than love as God loves, the wicked man destroys it, and seeks to go his own way. With no knowledge of God comes no love for God's law, and so mankind descends into these sins from the moment of conception. We are indeed a cursed race.

But it doesn't end there. Paul continues, an ever-expanding list of the evils of man. 'Slanderers'. Watch even seemingly kind, warm-hearted people explode when they are wronged. Watch outwardly good politicians tear their opponents down. The media, retail, a thousand places and examples show that slander seems to be a monster in the most kind-hearted of people, and the primary difference between people is the manner in which it is revealed. And if this slander is aimed towards men, then surely it will then turn against the One whose truth they have forsaken.

Indeed, Paul labels the sinful man a God-hater. This is no mere apathy, like many try to say. When a person is infinitely glorious, and of infinite value, anything short of devotion is hatred. A man who turns his back on God, and rejects His truth and the knowledge of Him, is not merely someone who chooses his own path. He is a hater of God, someone who spits at divine glory and walks away in disgust. Surely his destruction is well deserved.

Think of the Cross in light of this. How great is the love of God! Yet men continue pridefully in their sins! They are insolent, arrogant and boastful. They have no shame, they revel in their wickedness, flaunting in it. They invent ways of doing evil, for their desire for wickedness is never quenched; they forever want more, and so they continually seek new ways to curse God. And one of the most fundamental of these is to reject one's parents, the models of godly leadership in the home. Parents are the primary shapers of a person's future. They make or break everything. And if a child rebels against his parents blatantly, he will rebel against anything and everything. Parents are the first illustration of God that a child has. If they are rejected, there are dire consequences. God's created order is despised, and so is He.

Once men have been filled with wickedness against God and man, and grown insolent and proud in their sins, they lose all sensitivity. Ezekiel 36:26-27 promises that, under the New Covenant given by the Christ, believers will be given a new heart and the indwelling Spirit so that they will be sensitive to God's will and follow it. Romans 1:31 shows why a new heart is so essential for that. Embracing sin, the natural man becomes senseless in the things of God.

He has no concept of God's authority or laws, and so lives in rebellion without regard for any warnings. "It's my body", "it's my lifestyle", "keep out of my bedroom", etc, are what the sinner cries when confronted with his crimes, and he gives no thought to the God he offends.

After all, he is faithless, deprived of the one thing that can save him. So he drifts, becoming more and more heartless as his whole being is consumed with a drive for self-satisfaction at the expense of anything and anyone around him. He becomes ruthless in this pursuit, and will stop at nothing to achieve it. Helping an old lady across the street becomes a selfish exercise, as does a successful doctor who simply wants to satisfy his desire to do right. Without an aim to the glory of God, these things all become empty and selfish. This is the human heart, and it is deceitful and wicked beyond measure (Jeremiah 17:9). Only God can save us from this. That is why we so desperately need His Gospel.

At the end of passage, Paul completes his treatment of the depth of man's sin and rebellion. Here he makes one damning statement to conclusively sum up and demonstrate the guilt of every man. This is done in two ways. First, he shows that God's moral standards are written on every human heart. They know God's righteous decree, they know within their hearts that what they do is beyond justifying. They stand naked before the Throne of Judgement with no alibi of ignorance. "They exchanged the truth of God for a lie", verse 25 declared, and so in their arrogance they cast aside truth and what they know to be right.

And they do not warn the wicked: no, instead they also approve of those who practice them. The greatest sinners are the greatest heroes. As long as someone achieves what their society or group calls "success" in any area, their sin is either ignored or celebrated. This is common across all societies, all people groups. And these two demonstrations of man's guilt Paul looks upon with horror. He looks across the devastated wasteland of mankind and, as Romans 9:23 reveals, he weeps. Like Jeremiah, like Isaiah, like Jesus, Paul looks at rebellion and the hatred of God and he weeps. These verses of condemnation are why he preaches the Gospel of God, the proclamation of a righteousness that is not our own.

Can there be any question? Our race needs a saviour. Only Jesus Christ can fill that role.

The Universality of Damnation

Romans 3:10-18

"None is righteous, no, not one;

no one understands;

no one seeks for God.

All have turned aside; together they have become worthless;

no one does good, not even one."

"Their throat is an open grave;

they use their tongues to deceive."

"The venom of asps is under their lips."

"Their mouth is full of curses and bitterness."

"Their feet are swift to shed blood;

in their paths are ruin and misery,

and the way of peace they have not known."

"There is no fear of God before their eyes."

Here Paul begins a series of quotes from the Psalms to explain the total depravity of man he has just detailed. This is the summary of his argument, the description of every unbeliever. This first quotation seems to be drawn from Psalm 14:1, an overarching, damning conviction of man. Many ask what the fate is of the innocent man who has never heard the Gospel. According to Paul, the answer is, as David Platt puts it, "That man undoubtedly goes to Heaven...the only problem is, that guy does not exist" (2010).

As Paul declares, there is no one righteous, not even one. The key to understanding the Gospel is to understand that man is inherently unrighteous, and evil.

Paul goes on to say that no one understands. God is revealed in nature, and yet history has proven time and again that men are much more likely to worship the created than the creator. For all their distress at the 'human condition', people still fail to grasp God's righteous standards, for they still grasp at the 'good' they think they see in people. The things of God are not understood by men, and so no one seeks God.

Every man wants love, but few want it from someone who threatens to damn them.

Everyone wants joy, but few want to gain it by sorrow.

Every man wants the gifts of God, but dig deep enough, and you'll find that everyone hates the God who gives these gifts.

Most Christians cannot accept the doctrine of predestination, thinking that it reveals an evil God. How can the unsaved believe in Him if the saved struggle? Truth be told, most suffer from this lack of perception and understanding, not just one group. But if the sinner does not truly seek God, how can he be saved? The painful truth is this: only God can save. We are instruments of His mercy, but only God can soften the heart that hates Him.

We speak of great men, noble men, awe-inspiring humanitarians. But the simple truth is that without the grace of God in Jesus Christ, even Mother Theresa deserved to burn in Hell. For in their sins, all men have become worthless.

I have heard preachers say that God wants to save sinners so He can fulfil their dreams. This is lunacy, for their dreams are worthless, sinful, selfish. I have also heard preachers say that God saves men because He needs them for His plans to be fulfilled. This is blasphemy. God has no need of worthless men for His plans to be fulfilled. He saves men for His good pleasure.

And the fact that a holy God would do such a thing should leave us in awe. He is pure, righteous, transcendent, immutable, holy, and of man it is said, there is no one who does good, not even one. Apart from the saving work of Christ, the most humanitarian work is, at its very core, horrifying sin, primarily rooted in either disgusting pride or God-hating humanism. Should God desire the company of beings who are utterly incapable of doing good? The astounding fact of the matter is, He does.

Dear Christian, do not see yourself as above the depraved masses depicted here. We, indeed, were once lost in such miserable darkness (Ephesians 2:3), and yet the Holy One showed Himself to be the God of Mercy on our behalf. And how perverted we once were! See the corruption of men's lips! James says that the tongue steers a man's life (3:5-12), and where can the depraved tongue lead but a fiery Hell? Open graves, practicing deceit, is the state of our tongues. They kill, they defile, they deceive. The poison of vipers drips off and paralyses, maims, kills, those around us.

This was once us, dear Christian! Many of us still have not learnt the horror of the human tongue. We have thought so much on grand speeches that we have forgotten the horror we are capable of speaking, the death that the mouth can deliver.

When a mouth is full, nothing is added. If our mouths are full of cursing and bitterness, then life-giving speech will not live long therein. What a horrifying thought! And yet, this we once were, enslaved to such horror! So too are the non-Christians we set up as our idols. Only Christ can purify our hearts, our lives, our tongues. Out of the overflow of the heart the mouth speaks (Matthew 12:34), and how can good flow from a depraved, God-hating heart? And yet men with such unholy, filth-ridden, mouths are saved and forgiven by God on a daily basis. Marvel at the mercy of God, for it is beyond comparison, and beyond comprehension.

See here man's lust for violence. Not only is it the path he takes to acquire his personal gain, he is swift to take it. How true is this! Men will come to violent blows over theology, sporting teams, music tastes. It is unknown why Hitler had the Jews slaughtered. The very existence of the possibility of such evil in a man should make one tremble, and he was hardly the worst even in recent history. Human beings are so desperately wicked, so frighteningly eager in selfishness, that violence and murder are constantly legitimate options in our minds.

Indeed, ruin and misery is the trail we leave behind as we journey through life. How many hearts are broken, how many families are left shattered in even the best of neighbourhoods in the best of countries? Every selfish choice we make damages another life, no matter how minor or insignificant it may seem. Christ came to save the worst scum in existence. Our legacies prove that we are those scum, no matter how 'good' they seem. Without Christ, every lasting legacy is built on destruction of others. Ruin and misery mark their ways. Can we truly look at ourselves and say that we are different? If you can, you're lying, or you don't understand.

When Paul goes on to speak of "the way of peace", he's not talking of some 'inner peace' given by self-help gurus. No, he speaks of the way of peace given by God alone, that harkens back to the Garden of Eden, when no strife existed, no conflict marred the earth. We see this in the bond between two Christians who disagree on some point of doctrine that brings them to loggerheads, and yet they love each other and will die for each other. This is a peace that cannot truly be known apart from God.

Every other path of 'peace' caters to our own selfish desires, and 'one-size-fits-all' is a lie. Yet with God, there is one way - Jesus Christ. Ultimately, this is peace with God. Without this way of peace, we are at war with God, and damnation is our lot. This is the way of peace they do not know. They do not know the Cross. That is their destruction.

Without Christ, men are blind. We cannot see God as beautiful, or holy, or righteous. We can only look upon Him with contempt and hatred. Truly think on the attributes of God, Christian. Would you really love Him had He not given you a new heart? The unregenerated, natural man has no reverence of God. Can you truly fault God for damning a sinner? God is almighty, all-glorious, all-holy, all-beautiful, all-sovereign, and yet the average man pays Him no mind except, maybe, on Christmas or Easter. That is despicable. They are haters of God (Romans 1:30), and they know not the fear of God. What

hope, then, is there for them?

The End of Damnation

By this point, it is quite clear that mankind is sinful and deserving of God's hatred and wrath. We see the beginnings of this wrath in our sufferings and punishment on earth. We see it in sickness, in trials, in pain, in everyday agonies. But God has also decreed an everlasting punishment for those who do not turn to Him and repent.

Revelation 19:11 describes Jesus as the One who is Faithful and True to execute judgement and war on evil humanity. In verse 15, it is revealed that "He will tread the winepress of the fury of the wrath of God the Almighty." This is the entire force of the furious anger and hatred of an all-powerful being unleashed on humanity. This is an unquenchable thirst for vengeance on blasphemy and rebellion. This is unyielding annihilation of all opposition in one bloody swoop.

And yet, if this was not horrifying enough, the destruction brought about by the hatred of an Almighty God, we are then told that the result is not mere physical death or annihilation, but eternity being tortured by God Himself. Revelation 20:15 tells us that after this horrifying destruction, all the dead will be raised and judged. The wicked will be sentenced to a lake of fire, where "their worm shall not die, their fire shall not be quenched, and they shall be an abhorrence to all flesh" (Isaiah 66:24).

Romans 2:5 says, "But because of your hard and impenitent heart you are storing up wrath for yourself on the day of wrath when God's righteous judgment will be revealed."

This contempt comes from a man's stubbornness and unwillingness to repent. He refuses to yield himself to God, to surrender, and in his insolence continues in his sins. The result of this is terrifying: such a man is storing up wrath against himself. Note here who is storing up wrath. God is not levelling a cannon at an unsuspecting, innocent bystander. By every second he spends in rebellion, the sinner illustrates his deserving of destruction. Every breath that is not breathed for the glory of God is another justification for his damnation. And that day is coming soon. The day of God's wrath is fast approaching. It is established. It is set in stone. No thing and no person in Heaven or Hell or on earth can move it back or bring it forward even a nanosecond. Every moment, we are hurtling towards it at cataclysmic speeds.

Rebellion will end, and it will be a great and terrible day. For this is the day that, finally, God's righteous judgement will be revealed. Unlike the hypocrite, God judges only in truth. And this will be the day on which it shall be openly revealed. God already knows our steps, our choices, our fates. Our time for repentance is now, and He already knows the outcome.

The day of wrath is not for Him to make a case. That is done every second of a man's life. The day of wrath is for the execution of the appointed sentence. This is why we must "work out [our] salvation will fear and trembling" (Philippians 2:12). The day of wrath is coming, and we know not when.

The Salvation From Damnation

Humanity has rebelled against the authority of Almighty God, and invoked His hatred and wrath. We are, by nature, children of wrath (Ephesians 2:3), headed for an eternity of destruction. What hope could there possibly be for us?

This is why we so desperately need the Gospel, the Good News of Jesus Christ. Despite our filth and wickedness, God, in His infinite mercy and grace and compassion and kindness, still loves us. "For God so loved the world that he gave his only son that whoever believes in him should not perish but have eternal life" (John 3:16).

Jesus Christ, the Son of God, the second member of the Trinity, was born of a virgin, and lived a perfect, holy, sinless life. He was crucified on the Cross as a blood sacrifice to bear our sins, to make payment for our souls that we would be saved from our sins, and saved to a life of obedience. He then rose from the grave to show that the sacrifice had been accepted; to take His place as our Lord and King; and to assure us of the eternal life that He promises.

Our sins, our filth, our depravity, have separated us from God, the Holy One. But when we have faith in Christ, when we place our trust in His sacrifice upon that Cross, we can be saved. We can be redeemed, made anew. Made a new Creation. We are saved from the wrath of God by the grace of God.

It is not because of our effort, not because of our apparent goodness, not because of anything within us. As Romans 9 says, "it depends not on human will or exertion, but on God, who has mercy." We cannot save ourselves. It is only by the supernatural work of the Spirit of God.

This is the Gospel. This is our only hope.

May the Lamb that was slain receive the reward of His suffering.

Bibliography

MacArthur, J 2011. 'A Prophetic Message to an Ungodly Nation', sermon presented at Grace Community Church, California, June 26.

Platt, D 2010. 'What happens to those who never hear the Gospel', sermon presented at Southeastern Seminary, Wake Forest, North Carolina, 13 April

Ravenhill, L. 'A Burning Heart'.

Surrender Ministries

"Draw near to God, and he will draw near to you. Cleanse your hands, you sinners, and purify your hearts, you double-minded."

- James 4:8

God is calling all men everywhere to repent of their sins and trust in Jesus Christ for salvation. Throughout the world, this Gospel is being proclaimed by faithful men and women seeking to advance the Kingdom of God.

Surrender Ministries exists as an attempt to build up servants of Christ in their knowledge of, and devotion to, God. We believe that God rewards those who seek Him with more of Himself, and we desire to see many seek after Him.

God bless you, and may He use His servants for your growth and His glory. We are but vessels. May His Name be glorified.

www.facebook.com/surrenderministries7

Printed by Libri Plureos GmbH in Hamburg, Germany